# FOLK BRICK CARVING

# FOLK
# BRICK CARVING

*Compiled by Lan Xianlin*

FOREIGN LANGUAGES PRESS

First Edition 2008

ISBN 978-7-119-04672-3

©Foreign Languages Press, Beijing, China, 2008

*Published by*

Foreign Languages Press

24 Baiwanzhuang Road, Beijing 100037, China

http://www.flp.com.cn

*Distributed by*

China International Book Trading Corporation

35 Chegongzhuang Xilu, Beijing 100044, China

P.O. Box 399, Beijing, China

*Printed in the People's Republic of China*

# Contents

# Rooftop Brick Carving / 93

Main Ridge Brick Carving / 94
Sloping Ridge Brick Carving / 99

# Stucco Sculpture / 101

# Glaze / 125

INTRODUCTION

Brick carving is an art form widely applied in architectural decor in China. Using brick as the basic material and based on pottery and the art of stone carving, it features both the exquisite and the simple, imbuing a harmonious ambience on brick buildings. This form of art may be traced back to the 7th century BC, and has been perfected step by step in both craft and content through the ages.

Square brick with rinceau motifs, Warring States Period (474-221 BC), unearthed in Fenghuangtai, Shandong Qingzhou City Museum collection

## History

Brick carving originated out of early production and application of bricks, and evolved during its course. There were three main types of bricks in ancient times: square, strip and hollow. Square bricks were mostly decorated with motifs and usually used for paving floors. Strip bricks, also known as small bricks, were used for building water channels and for lining tomb chambers in earlier times. Only gradually did they begin to be used for building houses. Hollow bricks were mostly oblong in shape and hollow inside, mostly used for lining tomb chambers. Ancient bricks left over from cultural ruins are of great value in studying the development of the art of brick carving, as they are all engraved with the year of manufacture in addition to auspicious words or designs.

Hollow brick incised with dragon design, Qin Dynasty (221-206 BC), Shaanxi Provincial Museum of History collection

Brick with image of greeting guests, Han Dynasty (206 BC-AD 220), Shaanxi Provincial Museum of History collection

Square brick with lotus design, Tang Dynasty (618-907), Shaanxi Provincial Museum of History collection

Square brick with peach design, Han Dynasty (206 BC-AD 220), Handan City Museum collection, Hebei Province

Bricks carved with images of warriors, Song Dynasty (960-1279), Shaanxi Provincial Museum of History collection

Bricks were used as building materials in China a long, long time ago. The bricks unearthed from the ruins of the late Zhou period （1046-256 BC） in Shaanxi show that bricks appeared in China in around the 8th century BC, when they were used for paving floors. Strip and hollow bricks appeared in the 7th to 3rd centuries BC, when brick carving also appeared as evident in such motifs as 米 (rice), rope and fret.

In the 2nd century BC, a type of very solid brick, popularly known as the "lead brick," came into being in Lishan during the Qin Dynasty (221-206 BC), with the clay containing all types of minerals, which reinforced the bricks after being fired. During this period, decorative motifs were engraved on the basis of impressed molding. These motifs included rope, fret, circle, rhomb, S and cloud. The hollow bricks with dragon designs unearthed from Xianyang, the capital of the Qin Dynasty in Shaanxi, featured robust and in-depth composition and exquisite workmanship. They are the finest of the carved bricks of the Qin Dynasty.

With the perfection in shapes, brick carving also developed greatly. Such motifs as geometric designs, animal designs, auspicious words and

Introduction

combination of other designs appeared in the square, strip and hollow bricks unearthed from the ruins of the 2nd century BC to 2nd century AD. In fashion during this period was the use of the carved bricks and stones in mausoleums, especially during the Eastern Han period (AD 25-220). Such carved bricks are mainly found in Sichuan and Henan provinces. Following the tradition of impressed molding, the workmanship became even better than in previous dynasties. Subjects covered were more practical, with content including legends, labor, life, environment, natural landscapes, historical stories and personal biographies. The composition was well designed with appropriate density, and the images lively.

Carved bricks used to line tomb chambers in the 5th to 6th centuries were often painted in colors, with the subject matter of the designs covering literati, musicians and warriors as well as myths and religious tales. The application of carved bricks was extended to building Buddhist pagodas during this period. Glaze appeared as early as in the IIth century BC, brought in from the western regions, and had not been used in architecture until this period.

Brick carved with a dancer, Northern Song Dynasty (960-1127), Shaanxi Provincial Museum of History collection.

Long bricks carved with the date of manufacture, Jin Dynasty (265-420), Qingzhou City Museum collection, Shandong Province

Brick carved with a design of
a lady offering tea to another lady,
Northern Song Dynasty,
Shaanxi Provincial Museum of
History collection

From 7th to 10th centuries, bricks began to be used for the outer coverings of city walls, indicating the increase in output. During this period, carving was done on bricks after they were molded, which made the works more exquisite and more three-dimensional. During the Tang Dynasty (618-907), bricks with floral designs caught on in the paving of floors. Historical data reveals that the front part of the North Hall of the Tang-dynasty Cabinet Building was paved with bricks involving such floral designs as lotus and honeysuckle, which could be laid in continuous lines to make the floor more beautiful. Of the floral bricks of that period extant today, those in the Daming Palace and at Dunhuang are the most valuable. The carved bricks used to build the Xiuding Temple in Anyang, Henan Province, are the best examples of the period. There are more than 3,440 of them, with 72 designs including attendant maids, children, blue dragon, white tiger and Buddhist and Taoist figures.

Full brick structured buildings appeared from the late 10th century to the late 13th century. There was also major progress in the carving of bricks. The book *Methods and Style of Building* standardized the process of brick carving. The full carving method replaced the original impressed molding or carvings based on impressed molding. In addition, brick carving acquired the symbolic significance of grades, with standards for different grades. The carved bricks of the Song Dynasty (960-1279), unearthed in Yanshi of Henan Province, recorded the daily life of women, with the figurines carved with superb workmanship and in such innovative styles craftsmen made the figurines more vivid and expressive. The carved bricks lining the chamber of the Tomb of Dong in Houma, and the Tomb of Jin in Jishan in Shanxi Province, represent the highest level of brick carving in the 12th to 13th centuries, featuring bold shapes and well-laid out conception, including content such as the tomb's owner, servants, tales of piety, warriors, flowers, birds and animals carved in alto-relievo.

Screen wall, Ming Dynasty (1368-1644), Songjiang, Shanghai

Toward the end of the 14th century, carved bricks began to decorate such high-grade buildings as princely residences and temples. After the 16th century, stone carving and glaze replaced carved bricks in decorating high-grade buildings, with carved bricks downgraded. Such carved bricks, however, were extensively used in small residential houses. As the economy flourished, and with social stability, carved bricks were to be found everywhere. With the renewal of brick carving methods, the craft became more refined and its subject matter extended more widely, thus bringing about a golden age in the art of brick carving. After the 14th century, brick carvers were divided into different schools, such as Huizhou brick carving, Suzhou brick carving, Guangdong brick carving, Hezhou brick carving, and Beijing brick carving.

Influenced by baroque and rococo in the 18th to 19th centuries, building decoration became more elaborate. Toward the end of the 19th century, decorative carving grew stronger and the craft tended to become more minute and complicated, often seen in door heads, gable-wall heads, front-porch walls and screen walls. Stucco

Architectural brick carved with two gold fish, Qing Dynasty (1644-1911), Guangzhou

sculpture, an art form derived from brick carving, also emerged and gained great popularity in the coastal areas south of the Lingnan Mountains, making the local architecture more bright and colorful. Glaze became so dignified that it became a signature of imperial architecture and, outside the imperial family, could be used only in temples.

At this time, the variety of decorative motifs on carved bricks was also enriched. They included human figures, deities, auspicious birds and animals, flowers, grasses, mountains and rivers, utensils, silk motifs, and symbols. Brick carving also adopted the most popular forms, such as the use of metaphor, comparison and homophonic sounds to convey good wishes and fortune. For instance, the peach was used to represent long life; the peony to represent nobility; the pomegranate to express good wishes for more children; and the sheep was used to express piety. Plum, orchid, bamboo and chrysanthemum were used as similes for noble virtues; lotus was used to express cleanliness; the bat to homophonically signify happiness; deer homophonically to imply earnings; the chicken for its sound as luck. The themes of decorative brick carving fell into three major categories: wishes for happiness and fortune; the promotion of good morality and ethics; and exorcism of evil and disaster. The first category was the most widely applied, as a totality for happiness, earnings, long life, good tidings and wealth. All these are expressed in simple artistic language: the concerns of people for the value of life, their wishes for the rise of families, their pursuit of wealth and a happy life, and for their own social status. The subjects reflected the traditional way of thinking of the common people, their cultural concepts and their moral codes.

# Brick Carving Process

Brick carving is the art of bricks. Bricks are made of clay adobe fired at high temperatures, featuring resistance against wear and moisture, and for easy workability. There are green bricks, red bricks and tiles for flooring, depending on the raw material used and the ways of firing. Stucco sculpture is a derivative of brick carving. Glaze is a process in contrast to brick carving.

The process of the folk art of brick carving involves *shaohuo*, *shao*, chiseling, emboss and stucco emboss.

Screen-wall brick carving, Yangjiafu, Weifang, Shandong Province

*Shaohuo* is a most ancient process. Clay is molded into an abode by sculpturing or impressed molding and then put into a kiln for firing. It features ease in working, and low cost. However, the level of this process is low and rough.

*Shao* is a type of carving on the basis of firing work. It is more time consuming. Yet the finished products have sharp edges and clear layers, suitable for close-up viewing.

Chiseling mean applying a chisel directly on the brick. It has a variety of methods, and the products are expressive.

Emboss is a sub-system of brick carving, using emboss and engraving techniques.

Stucco emboss is a method of mixing fine lime with fibrous plaster which is sculptured into a shape on the surface of bricks, mostly in shallow bold relief. The method is mostly used to decorate screen walls, eave walls, gable walls, doors and windows and roof ridges, featuring fresh styles and simplicity.

Brick carved with rinceau design,
Guangdong guild hall, Luodai,
Sichuan Province

Garden architectural brick carving,
Jiading, Shanghai

Peony screen-wall glaze, Longxing Temple,
Zhengding, Hebei Province

Theatrical figures, stucco sculpture,
Guandi Temple, Dongshan, Fujian Province

Glazed animal, Jingzhou,
Hubei Province

Stucco sculpture on door head,
Zhongxian County, Chongqing

*Introduction*

# Regional Styles of Brick Carving

Brick carving is widespread in China, especially in Beijing, Tianjin, Shandong, Shanxi, Shaanxi, Anhui, Jiangsu and Guangdong. Brick carvings in different places feature different styles, and have evolved into different schools of the art. The most famous are Huizhou brick carving, Suzhou brick carving, Guangdong brick carving and Hezhou brick carving.

Peony, brick carving, Baiyunguan Temple, Beijing

Beijing brick carving. Beijing, serving as a capital for several dynasties, was noted for its tight control by the feudal patriarchal system. Glaze and color paintings could only be used to decorate imperial palaces, temples and other large structures. Brick carving developed only among the common people for decorating houses. It was widely applied in enclosed courtyard houses. Beijing brick carving had its heyday during the Qing Dynasty (1644-1911). The craft was mature and carving methods included bold relief, openwork and line engraving. Subject matter covered mainly flowers, with strict styles, composed and bold, mainly used to decorate screen walls, door heads, eave walls, and front-porch walls.

Brick carving of Chinese character "fu" (happiness), Shi Family Compound, Yangliuqing of Tianjin

Tianjin brick carving. Tianjin used to be a major seaport of China in the 17th to 20th centuries, where all the rich merchants and nobilities gathered. In order to show off their riches, they vied with one another to build luxurious houses decorated with carved bricks. The brisk market demand stimulated the development of this trade. Tianjin brick carving is refined, featuring circular carving, relief carving and line engraving. Subject matter included quite stylish figures, auspicious fowls and animals as well as flowers. The carving is minute and complicated in style. At the beginning of the 19th century, brick carvers Ma Shunqing and Ma Shaoqing (father and son) created a new method. By piecing and plastering, they succeeded in making brick carving more stratified, suitable for large brick works.

Door brick carving,
Weixian County, Hebei Province

Weixian brick carving. This is a type of carving popular in the Weifang area of Shandong Province. It stresses arrangement, conception and exaggerated shape. Designs mainly feature auspicious animals and flowers. The style is bold and simple, with strong local color.

Shanxi brick carving. Shanxi brick carving had its glorious prime in the 12th to 13th centuries. It reached its heyday by the mid-1700, when the society was stable, economy prospered. Rich merchants, particularly from Anhui and Shanxi, began to build their magnificent houses by using the best materials. It was most popular in the central part of Shanxi, where merchants gathered. Shanxi brick carving belongs to the northern school of art, featuring skill, exquisite craft, rich conception, and complexity. Subject matter mostly concentrated on happiness, earnings, long life, good tidings and wealth. It was mainly used to decorate screen walls, door heads, eave walls, steps, pediments and roof ridges.

Front-porch wall brick carving,
Dingcun Village of Xiangfen, Shanxi Province

Brick carving of Chinese character of "Longevity," Dingcun Village of Xiangfen, Shanxi Province

Shanxi brick carving. The history of Shaanxi brick carving is long. It carried forward the styles from the prime of the Tang Dynasty (7th-8th centuries) and absorbed the strong points of brick carving of Shanxi and Gansu, while developing a style of its own, featuring skill, rich conception, traditional and simple plastering, as well as magnificence. Designs include figures, animals and flowers, all conveying the message of good luck.

Gansu brick carving. The home of Gansu brick carving is Linxia, which was known as Hezhou in ancient times, which is why Gansu brick carving is also called "Hezhou brick carving." Gansu brick carving experienced great development in the 12th to 13th centuries, as evidenced by the objects unearthed from ancient tombs. There are two ways of doing the carving. One is to mold the clay into adobe and put it into a kiln to fire. Another is to fire the adobe first and then do the carving. Gansu brick carving is mature, with delicate workmanship. Designs include the dragon, phoenix, lion, tiger, worm, bird and flower. The carvings were widely applied to decorate temples and screen walls, gate entrances, as well as footpaths and gable walls of ordinary houses.

Huizhou brick carving. Huizhou brick carving is the most famous. Ancient Huizhou was in the southern part of today's Anhui Province. Its commerce was very developed by the 14th to 19th centuries. Wallowing in great riches, Huizhou merchants began to build elaborate houses, gardens and temples. Rivals in ostentation, they vied with one another to invite the best designers and carvers to decorate their structures. This stimulated a rapid development of wood, stone

Door-head brick carving, Shexian County, Anhui Province

Door-head brick carving, Suzhou

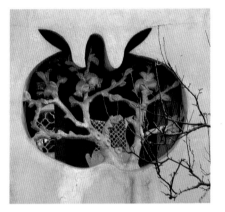

Pomegranate, stucco sculpture,
Canglang Pavilion, Suzhou

Rooftop brick carving,
Yangzhou, Jiangsu Province

and brick carving. Huizhou brick carving used polished black bricks, noted for their fine texture and a variety of finishing touches. Often, the main object in the front is carved in circular relief, with the background carved in several layers of bold relief, and objects in the middle in openwork. The subject matter of designs includes figures, animals, flowers, landscapes, and auspicious graphics and symbols.

Suzhou brick carving. Suzhou is well known for its brick carving in China. The brick-making industry began to develop uninterrupted from the 14th century. From 1506 to 1522, the square bricks of the imperial kiln in Suzhou were renowned as "gold brick" for their metal-like quality and texture. The production of such bricks continued into the 17th century, mainly used as materials for carving. Suzhou brick carving matured in the 18th century, when the craft reached its consummate level. The designs appeared more three-dimensional and the composition more beautiful, bright and more harmonious, with subject matter covering figures, animals, flowers, landscapes and auspicious graphics and symbols, and styles more elegant and graceful.

Window brick carving, Foshan,
Guangdong Province

Guangdong brick carving. Guangdong brick carving is mainly produced in Shawan and Foshan. Shawan brick carving was in vogue through the 14th to 19th centuries, even having some impact on Southeast Asian countries. Guangdong brick carving is noted for its variety of techniques, including high relief, shallow relief and circular engraving, sometimes combined with color painting, clay sculpture and stucco sculpture. Finished products include both single pieces and composite pieces. They feature in-depth composition, strong three-dimensional effect and multifarious styles, with designs covering legends, auspicious fowls as well as animals and flowers. They are mainly used to decorate screen walls, eave walls, gable-wall heads, wall heads and the niches of family and other temples.

Door-head brick carving,
Chen Clan Ancestral Hall, Guangzhou

In general, brick carving in northern China is noted for its skillful craft, compact plastering and simple and bold style, while that of southern China is noted for the variety of techniques, exquisite designs and three-dimensional effect, as well as their elegant style and more feminine beauty.

Fire-wall brick carving, Liu Family Manor, Dayi, Sichuan Province

Two dragons playing with a ball, stucco sculpture, Cai Clan Ancestral Hall, Quanzhou, Fujian Province

Two dragons playing with a ball, wall-face stucco sculpture, Zitong, Sichuan Province

Brick carving for decorating ridges, Yichang, Hubei Province

Eave-wall stucco sculpture, Zhongxian County, Chongqing

# SCREEN WALL BRICK CARVING

# Screen Wall Brick Carving

The screen wall is an isolated wall either outside or inside the gate of a traditional Chinese house. A screen wall inside the entrance of a house is often built to block the view of passersby, and to decorate the courtyard. In ancient times, it was part of the system of the rite. A screen wall outside the gate indicates high-grade architecture, for which only the king of a state was qualified to have built in the Spring and Autumn Period (770-476 BC).

Brick carving for screen walls is mainly applied to decorate the top, eave, base (of Buddhist images and of Buddhist pagodas) and the center of the screen wall, giving greater prominence to the center. There are two types of composition. One is regular composition, which uses lines or motifs to form a square, on which square bricks are placed, with floral designs at the four corners and a bigger floral design in the center. Composition is free in style, without being confined to any particular rules, just as in painting. Subjects of screen-wall brick carvings cover a wide range, including auspicious words such as those indicating happiness, wealth and longevity and good tidings, as well as figures, animals and flowers symbolizing good luck.

## Detached Screen Wall

A detached screen wall is erected either outside a courtyard at a place opposite the gate or hidden inside the entrance to block the view of passersby.

The happiness and longevity motif, screen-wall brick carving,
Wang Family Compound, Shanxi

Screen-wall brick carving, Yangcheng, Shanxi

Screen-wall brick carving, Dingcun Village,
Xiangfen, Shanxi

Screen-wall brick carving,
Grand Mosque, Xi'an

Screen-wall brick carving,
Wang Family Compound, Shanxi

Design of five bats surrounding the
character for "longevity," conveying a
message of luck, screen-wall brick carving,
Pingyao, Shanxi

Tiger from the mountain, screen-wall brick carving,
Songjiang, Shanghai

Peony, symbol of nobility, screen-wall brick carving,
Xicheng District, Beijing

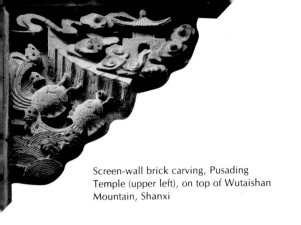

Screen-wall brick carving, Pusading
Temple (upper left), on top of Wutaishan
Mountain, Shanxi

Screen-wall brick carving, Pusading
Temple (upper right), on top of Wutaishan
Mountain, Shanxi

Islamic writing, central floral design of screen wall,
Grand Mosque in Xi'an

Wild geese in clouds, brick carving at
the corners of the screen wall, Xichang
District, Beijing (lower right)

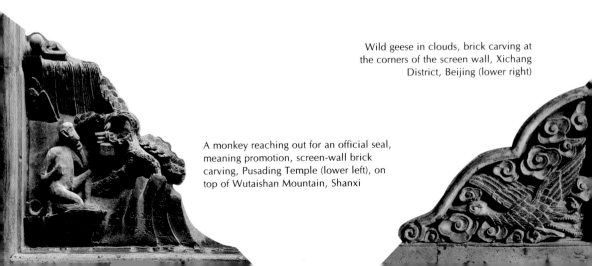

A monkey reaching out for an official seal,
meaning promotion, screen-wall brick
carving, Pusading Temple (lower left), on
top of Wutaishan Mountain, Shanxi

## Qilin Bringing Luck

Qilin, also spelt as Kylin, is considered one of the four most intelligent animals in Chinese culture, together with the Dragon, Phoenix and Tortoise. It looks like a deer with a single horn. Legend has it that a qilin appeared with a heavenly book when Confucius was born. In Chinese mythology, its appearance often coincides with an imminent birth. So the baby is often called "a child of qilin," who will have a bright future.

Qilin bringing luck, screen-wall brick carving, Songjiang, Shanghai

## Grand Duke Jiang Fishing Without Bait

Grand Duke Jiang, or Jiang Tai Gong, served as an official under the last king of the Shang Dynasty in the 11th century BC. He came to hate the tyrannical and debauched slave-owner who spent his days carousing with his favorite concubines, while mercilessly executing or punishing upright officials and others who opposed him. One day, when Jiang was fishing by a river (using a rod but with neither hook nor bait), he happened to meet King Wen of Zhou. He then assisted King Wen in overthrowing the tyrannical king of the Shang Dynasty and founded the Western Zhou (11th century BC to 771 BC). The story later became a folktale, conveying the message that, "If you just wait long enough, things will come your way."

Grand Duke Jiang Fishing Without Bait, screen-wall brick carving,
Puhua Temple, Wutaishan Mountain, Shanxi

Subduing dragons, screen-wall brick carving, Puhua Temple,
Wutaishan Mountain, Shanxi

Central flower brick carving,
Baiyunguan Temple, Beijing

One Hundred Birds Singing Praises of the Phoenix,
screen-wall brick carving, Baomoyuan, Fanyu, Guangdong

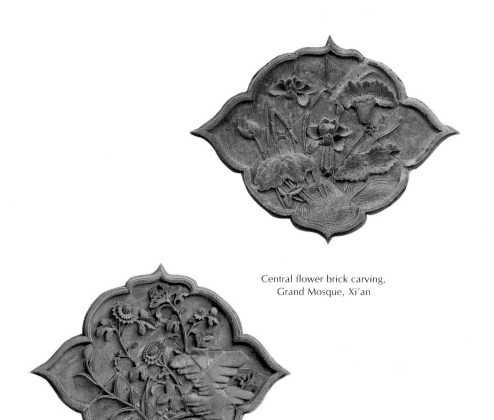

Central flower brick carving,
Grand Mosque, Xi'an

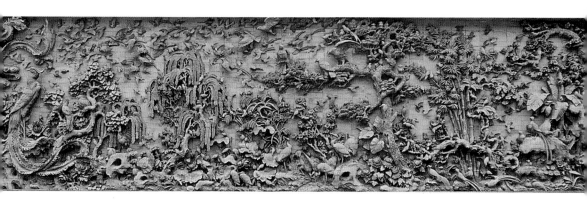

Carp Leaping over the Dragon Gate, screen-wall brick carving,
Jingshengzhen, Lingshi, Shanxi

## Carp Leaping over the Dragon Gate

The composition shows carps swimming against the torrent, trying to leap over the
dragon gate to become flying dragons. "Dragon gate" is a symbol of fame and glory.
The picture conveys the message of candidates passing the imperial examination and
going all the way up to high official positions.

## Wall-attached Screen Wall

A screen wall attached to a gable wall or a courtyard wall has similar styles with the main structures, forming part of the building complex.

Screen-wall brick carving, Grand Mosque, Xi'an

Screen-wall brick carving, Chenghuang Temple, Sanyuan, Shanxi

Screen-wall brick carving, Grand Mosque, Xi'an

Chinese character "净," for pureness, screen-wall brick carving, Grand Mosque, Xi'an

Pines and bamboo, screen-wall brick carving, Ci'en Temple, Xi'an

Bodhi and lotus, screen-wall brick carving, Ci'en Temple, Xi'an

*Bogu* design screen-wall brick carving, Grand Mosque, Xi'an

## DOOR AND WINDOW
## BRICK CARVING

# Door and Window Brick Carving

## Door Brick Carving

A door or a gate is an architectural facade and also a place where brick carvers may display their talent. Carvings are done mainly on the door head and lintel. The door head, also called a door cover, is a canopy-like structure over the door to protect the door from sun and rain. The lintel is a horizontal beam over the door. Traditionally, the lintel is usually a wooden structure. The use of brick carving to imitate woodcarving looks no less elegant than a wood carved lintel.

Rinceau motif, arched-door brick carving,
Grand Mosque, Xi'an

Door-head brick carving,
Grand Mosque, Xi'an

Door-head, moon gate brick carving, Grand Mosque, Xi'an

Door-head brick carving, Yuyuan Garden, Shanghai

Door-head brick carving, Xitang, Zhejiang

Door-head brick carving, Mingshan Hall in Dongshan, Suzhou

## The Noble Peony

The peony is a most important flower symbolizing nobility, wealth and luck. It is, therefore, also called the "flower of wealth" in Chinese. Combined with a basket, it is known as "prosperous flower basket."

Noble peony, lintel brick carving, residential building,
Xicheng District, Beijing

Peony and rinceau, lintel brick carving, residential building,
Xicheng District, Beijing

Eternal Spring, lintel brick carving, residential building, Beijing

## Spring in All Four Seasons

The representation of the four seasons is made up of flowers and birds of the four seasons, such as narcissus, lotus, chrysanthemum and plum, or peony, lotus, chrysanthemum and plum. They express good wishes for eternal spring and a happy life.

## San Yang Kai Tai

"*San yang kai tai*" means the arrival of spring, an auspicious beginning of a new year. *San yang* in the Eight Diagrams is a symbol marking the end of winter and the beginning of spring. "*San yang kai tai*" is an auspicious greeting for the beginning of a year.

*San yang kai tai*, lintel brick carving, Jingdezhen, Jiangxi

Hehe Immortals, lintel brick carving, Sanshandao, Suzhou

## Hehe Immortals

Legend has it that the two immortals, Hanshan and Shide, were close friends who, without knowing it, were both in love with the same woman. When Hanshan discovered the truth, he shaved his head to become a monk. After learning about this, Shide also left the young woman to join Hanshan. The two later jointly built the Hanshan Temple. They were later known as Hehe (harmony and unity) Immortals. Their portraits used to be hung in the central hall during wedding ceremonies. The two appear as children, with one holding a lotus, and the other, a round box or a treasure box from which five bats are flying out, conveying a message of harmony and unity.

Lintel brick carving, Shexian County, Anhui

Lintel brick carving, Xidi,
Shexian County, Anhui

Lintel brick carving, Chengkan,
Shexian County, Anhui

Lintel brick carving, Qiankou,
Shexian County, Anhui

## Window Brick Carving

Typical of window bricks are carvings for a variety of windows and tracery windows. A variety of windows are often seen in the gardens of northern China. They include round, hexagonal, fan-shaped, plum-shaped, peach-shaped and pomegranate-shaped windows. Carving is mainly applied to the shell of the outer window frame. There is another window called the "sham window," with brick carving inlaid, impervious to light, which is mainly used to decorate wall faces. A tracery or lattice window is openwork, with delicate sash bars, unopenable, frequently seen in the gardens of southern China. Tracery windows are also available in a wide variety, often with the center or sill decorated with brick carvings. Tracery windows are exquisitely and poetically structured.

## Peony Design

Peony is considered the best of all flowers, dignified and graceful, representing national beauty and heavenly fragrance, symbolizing auspiciousness, riches and honor.

Peony design, arched-window brick carving,
Linji Temple, Zhengding, Hebei

## Swastika

The pattern is linked to the traditional swastika, which was a kind of incantation in ancient times, symbolizing luck and also a symbol of Buddhism. It conveys the message of eternal flow of luck.

## Persimmon calyx pattern

The pattern is like a persimmon calyx, either in the shape of a rhomb or square. It first appeared in color pottery and bronze ware. It is said that the persimmon represents seven virtues: long life, shade, no bird nests, no worms, appealing leaves, tasty fruit, and fallen leaves usable for writing. The continuous flow using such a pattern symbolizes that all is well.

Swastika pattern,
tracery-window brick carving,
Shi Family Compound, Yangliuqing, Tianjin

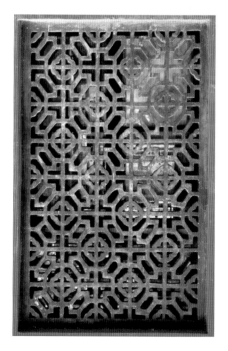

Persimmon calyx pattern,
tracery-window brick carving,
Tengwang Pavilion, Langzhong, Sichuan

Five bats design, tracery-window brick carving,
Yuyuan Garden, Shanghai

## Five Bats Design

The design depicts five bats flying around the Chinese character for "long life." To Chinese people, the bat is an animal signifying luck. According to the ancients, ideal happiness is a realm including long life, many children, riches, virtues and end of life. The design is often used for birthday celebrations.

Arched-window brick carving, Longxing Temple, Zhengding, Hebei

Two dragons playing with a ball,
tracery-window brick carving,
Yue Fei Temple, Hangzhou

## Two Dragons Playing with a Ball

The design depicts two dragons trying to catch a ball in the misty clouds. It is said that a dragon can spit out balls, which are called "dragon pearls." Dragons and dragon pearls both represent luck and prevention of flood and fire.

## Dharma

This wheel is like the wheel of a cart of ancient times. It is a symbol of Buddhism. It is said that there is an all-conquering Calkravartiraja (Chakra) in ancient India. When he was born, a Dharma appeared in the sky indicating that he would have no rival under Heaven.

Dharma, tracery-window brick carving,
Taihui Temple, Jingzhou, Hubei

Dragon design, tracery-window brick carving,
Jingci Temple, Hangzhou

## Openwork Brick Carving

Brick carving can prevent wood inside the walls from rotting. This is mostly used in northern China. It is oblong, round or hexagonal in shape. Designs are mainly plum, orchid, bamboo and chrysanthemum. There are also designs of lucky animals or words.

Peony, openwork brick carving,
Baiyunguan Temple, Beijing

Bamboo, openwork brick carving,
Baiyunguan Temple, Beijing

## Double-coin Pattern

The pattern is used to express wishes for wealth. Nine coins linked together indicate luck, as the numeral 9 in ancient China was regarded as a lucky number.

Double-coin pattern, openwork brick carving,
Wang family miniature garden, in Yangzhou, Jiangsu

Lotus, openwork brick carving,
Baiyunguan Temple, Beijing

Pompon (dahlia), openwork brick carving,
Baiyunguan Temple, Beijing

Fret pattern, openwork brick carving,
Chenghuang Temple, Sanyuan, Shaanxi

Phoenix and peony, openwork brick carving,
Xiaokong Cave, Qingyang, Gansu

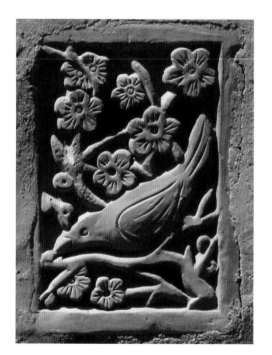

Magpie and plum, openwork brick carving,
Baiyunguan Temple, Beijing

# WALL-FACE BRICK
CARVING

# Wall-face Brick Carving

Wall faces are the main part of a house where brick carving is applied. There are several types of walls according to their positions: eave wall, front-porch wall, courtyard wall and gable wall.

## Eave-wall Brick Carving

The eave wall is the main site for brickwork decoration. Imitating wood carving, the patterns are usually continuous rinceau, covering a wide range of subjects.

The above pictures show the four branches of the arts that ancient men of letters were required to master: zither, chess, calligraphy, and painting.
Eave-wall brick carving, Qiao Family Compound, Qixian, Shanxi

*Bogu* pattern, eave-wall brick carving, Qiao Family Compound, Qixian, Shanxi

Picture of a boy, Liu Hai, playing with a string of coins and a toad,
said to be a God of Wealth, eave-wall brick carving, Qiao Family Compound, Qixian, Shanxi

Phoenix and peony, eave-wall brick carving,
Qiao Family Compound, Qixian, Shanxi

Grapes, a symbol for many children, eave-wall brick carving,
Qiao Family Compound, Qixian, Shanxi

Lotus and bird, eave-wall brick carving, Qiao Family Compound,
Qixian, Shanxi

Orchid and bamboo, eave-wall brick carving,
Qiao Family Compound, Qixian, Shanxi

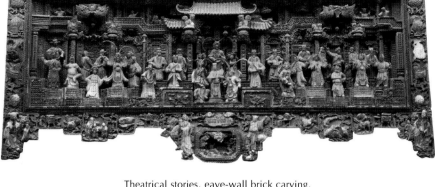

Theatrical stories, eave-wall brick carving,
Chen Clan Ancestral Hall, Guangzhou

Word pattern, eave-wall brick carving,
Cai family residence, Quanzhou, Fujian

Word pattern, eave-wall brick carving, Cai family residence, Quanzhou, Fujian

## Front-porch Wall Brick Carving

Walls on the two sides of the front porch under the extended front eave are often decorated with brickwork on the upper part. Decoration includes an oblong frame skirted with gadroon patterns, with bricks carved with patterns in the middle, resembling a scroll painting hanging on the wall. Stress is laid on a plain painting effect, with patterns done in low-relief carving, plain carving and inlay. Compositions include a regular pattern of flowers in the center plus flowers in the corners, but they are not confined to any particular pattern or patterns. Decorative subjects include figures, animals, flowers, grasses, writings and geometric patterns symbolizing luck.

Lucky fowls and animals, front-porch wall brick carving,
Cai family residence, Quanzhou, Fujian

*Bogu* design, front-porch wall brick carving, Cai family residence, Quanzhou, Fujian

## Bogu Design

This design includes bronze oven, porcelain vase, *ruyi*, gold bell, books, as well as calligraphy and paintings, sometimes with flowers and fruits alongside. Such design is often seen in the residences of scholars and officials.

Flowers and birds, front-porch wall brick carving,
Qiao Family Compound, Qixian, Shanxi

Chinese character meaning happiness,
front-porch wall brick carving,
Jade Emperor Pavilion, Pingluo,
Ningxia Hui Autonomous Region

Chinese character meaning remuneration,
front-porch wall brick carving, Jade Emperor
Pavilion, Pingluo, Ningxia

## Three Cold-resistant Plants

They refer to the pine tree, bamboo and plum. People often described men of virtue by comparing them to the three plants.

Pine, bamboo and plum, front-porch wall brick carving,
Grand Mosque, Xi'an

Front-porch wall brick carving,
Temple of Confucius, Shexian County, Anhui

Front-porch wall brick carving,
Shexian County, Anhui

## Courtyard-wall Brick Carving

Brick carving is done mainly on the top of the wall and the central part of the courtyard wall. There may be a whole section of brick carving or a combination of a number of brick carvings in the central part, especially on the courtyard walls of gardens and parks. The exquisite carving, set against the changing lattice windows and gates of different shapes, adds to the enchanting scene.

Courtyard-wall brick carving, former residence of Hu Xueyan, Hangzhou

Courtyard-wall brick carving, Mingshan Hall of Dongshan, Suzhou

## Five Generations Under One Roof

Five lions symbolize five generations, indicating people of five generations living under one roof. In ancient China, early marriages were common, and 20 years were regarded as one generation. People took pride in having people of five generations living under one roof, a sign of family harmony and prosperity.

Five generations under one roof, courtyard-wall brick carving, former residence of Hu Xueyan, Hangzhou

Design of Luan and Feng, courtyard-wall brick carving,
former residence of Hu Xueyan, Hangzhou

## Design of Luan and Feng

Both luan and feng are mythical birds, often living together peacefully. The design
symbolizes a happy couple.

Pattern of dragons in the form of rinceau, courtyard-wall brick carving,
former residence of Hu Xueyan, Hangzhou

Landscape design, courtyard-wall brick carving,
former residence of Hu Xueyan, Hangzhou

## Gable Wall Brick Carving

In southern China, people usually decorated the gable walls with a design of fish and grass, a symbol for preventing fire and disaster. In northern China, people also followed this practice and decorated the gable wall top with brick carvings of fish.

The gable wall head is a major place for brickwork decorations. Designs include all subjects conveying lucky meanings.

Pediment brick carving,
Dangjia Village of Hancheng, Shaanxi

## Composite Flower Design (*Bao Xian Hua*)

The design is made up of variations of peony, lotus, dahlia and other flowers in a radiating, symmetrical fashion. It prevailed during the Sui and Tang dynasties (6th-10th centuries). The design takes the sounds of the Chinese words *"bao"* and *"xian"* to imply treasure and immortal.

## Hanging Fish and *Recao* Design

Hanging fish is a decorative piece on the pediment of a gable wall. The design evolved from the bronze decor of the coffin cart in ancient times, and was adopted extensively to decorate palaces, temples and residential houses. *Recao* is a kind of seaweed. The design has a *ruyi* pattern at the end. The use of the design expresses the *fengshui* idea of using water to extinguish fire.

Hanging fish and *recao* design, pediment brick carving, Xiantong Temple,
Wutaishan Mountain, Shanxi

Composite flower design, pediment brick carving, Mosque at Dahuo Lane, Tianjin

Design with five bats flying around the
Chinese character for "longevity",
pediment brick carving, Shi Family Compound,
Yangliuqing, Tianjin

*Journey to the West*, pediment brick carving,
Banyuan Garden, Suzhou

Phoenix and peonies, pediment brick carving, Yangzhou

Design with five bats flying around the Chinese character for "longevity",
pediment brick carving, Zhuozheng Garden, Suzhou

### Aoyu

*Aoyu* is a gigantic fish, like a whale, that people used to worship in ancient times. It is said to have its origins in the makara of Indian mythology. But some people think it evolved from the whale. It is said that such fish can spit out water to extinguish fire. The use of the design is to express the wish to prevent fire and disaster.

*Aoyu*, gable-wall head brick carving, Huangling Temple, Yichang, Hubei

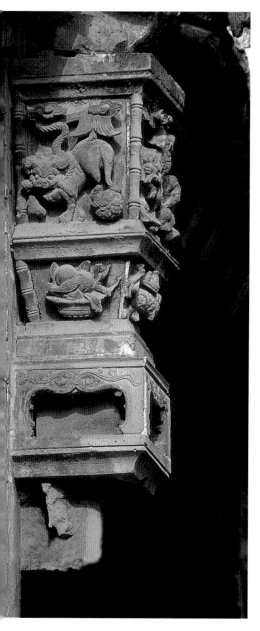

Lion and silk-threaded ball,
gable-wall head brick carving,
Dangjia Village in Hancheng, Shaanxi

Figures, gable-wall head brick carving,
Guozhuang, Hangzhou

## Qilin Bringing a Baby

It is a design of the mystical animal, Qilin, riding a cloud with a child on its back. In folk belief, Qilin is a kind animal that can bring children to people. Sincere worship of the animal is believed to help give birth to sons. That is why people call a son with benevolence, virtue and literary talent, a "son of Qilin."

## Lion Playing with a Ball

The design depicts a lion and a ball. The lion is the king of the beasts, ferocious and stately. People often used such design to drive away evil and keep the house peaceful. The ball represents luck. The lion and the ball combined symbolized official status and power. Other legends say that, when a male and a female lion play together, some of their hairs intertwine, forming a ball, from which lion cubs are born, thus symbolizing the proliferation and prosperity of family. The design evolved later on into the "lion-dance" often seen on festive occasions.

Qilin bringing a baby,
gable-wall head brick carving,
Dangjia Village in Hancheng, Shaanxi

Lion playing with a ball,
gable-wall head brick carving,
Dangjia Village in Hancheng, Shaanxi

Gable-wall head brick carving, Dangjia Village in Hancheng, Shaanxi

Flower and bird design,
gable-wall head brick carving,
Grand Mosque, Xi'an

Chrysanthemum design,
gable-wall head brick carving,
Shi Family Compound,
Yangliuqing, Tianjin

Lucky animals, gable-wall head brick carving,
Wolong Temple, Xi'an

Flower and bird design,
gable-wall head brick carving,
Grand Mosque, Xi'an

## Phoenix and Peony

Also known as "the phoenix playing with peony," the design features the legendary bird of fortune, the king of all birds, with the flower, peony, the king of all flowers, also known as the "noble flower." The two combined feature the theme of reproduction and luck, wealth and harmony.

Phoenix and peony,
gable-wall head brick carving,
Shi Family Compound,
Yangliuqing, Tianjin

Auspicious design,
gable-wall head brick carving,
Shi Family Compound,
Yangliuqing, Tianjin

Gable-wall head brick carving,
Chen Clan Ancestral Hall, Guangzhou

Five bats and longevity,
gable-wall head brick carving,
Shi Family Compound, Yangliuqing,
Tianjin

White-head bird and peony,
symbolizing a happy couple,
gable-wall head brick carving, Tianjin

Flower and bird design,
gable-wall head brick carving, Tianjin

Plum, bamboo and bird,
gable-wall head brick carving, Tianjin

Auspicious design,
gable-wall head brick carving, Tianjin

## Squirrel and Grapes

The grape, noted for the number of seeds inside, is often used to express wishes for more children. The squirrel is regarded as a deity for children. The combination of grape and squirrel symbolizes many children.

Squirrel and grapes, brick carving, residential house in Beijing

Lion playing with a ball,
brick carving, Beijing

Noble peony, brick carving, Beijing

Peony basket, brick carving, Beijing

ROOFTOP BRICK CARVING

# Rooftop Brick Carving

Materials used to decorate rooftops include tiles, brick carving, stucco sculpture, and glaze. Brick carving is mainly used to beautify the ridge and the roof corners with zodiac animals.

There is a full variety of brick carvings for decorating the ridge, which varies in style from place to place. In Shanxi and Shaanxi, the ornamentation is often supplemented by floral designs such as the peony, composite flower designs, and rinceau designs, looking striking but no less noble. Yet in southern China, the ridges are simple, with bird-like motifs on the ridge ends, and treasure vases or treasure troves on the center of the main ridge, beautiful and elegant in style.

## Main Ridge Brick Carving

The main ridge of a house had a dovetail at each end, which served as a joint of the main ridge and two diagonal ridges of a hip roof. As it was in a prominent place, a large and eye-catching dovetail was used to decorate the house.

Chinese character "fu" for happiness, main ridge motif, Ya'an, Sichuan

Lion, ridge motif, Qingyang, Gansu

Composite Flower design, main ridge brick carving,
Cao Family Compound in Taigu, Shanxi

## Dragon Dovetail

The dovetail is a decorative structure at the two ends of the main ridge. Its chief purpose is to fortify the roof structure. The dragon dovetail is shaped like a dragon, symbolizing that it can drive away fire and disaster.

Dragon dovetail motif, Huangling Temple,
Yichang, Hubei

Fish and dragon dovetail, Chongqing, Sichuan

## Fish and Dragon Dovetail

This is a dovetail for the main ridge, popular in southern China, shaped like both fish and dragon. It was used to decorate the ridge, symbolizing warding off disaster.

Gigantic Fish Dovetail, Qinglong Cave in Zhenyuan, Guizhou

Rinceau pattern for diagonal ridge for a hip roof, Chongqing, Sichuan

*Folk Brick Carving*

## Sloping Ridge Brick Carving

A house with sloping ridges extended from the main ridge on its two sides is of a high grade. There is a gargoyle-style dovetail at the lower end of such sloping ridge.

Rinceau pattern, main ridge brick carving,
Grand Mosque, Xi'an

## Chi Wen (legendary-animal-shaped dovetail)

*Chi* is a legendary animal that can extinguish fire. With its mouth open upward, it is posed as if swallowing the ridge, hence the name, "ridge-swallowing animal."

Main ridge gargoyle,
Wutaishan Mountain, Shanxi

*Chi Shou*, a legendary dragon, one of the nine sons of the dragon,
that can store a lot of water in its stomach, main ridge brick carving,
Qingyang Palace, Chengdu, Sichuan

STUCCO SCULPTURE

# Stucco Sculpture

Stucco sculpture is an integrated art, involving emboss, stucco sculpture and terracotta sculpture, extensively applied in architectural decor, especially in southern China. Stucco sculptures are frequently seen on roof ridges and on the top of walls in residential houses in places south of the Lingnan Mountains. Designs are complicated and elaborate and use strong contrasting colors. Sometimes, they are blended with some Western-style designs. In Fujian, seashells are used on the surface to make such sculptures shine.

*Fu, Lu, Shou* (happiness, wealth and longevity),
screen-wall stucco sculpture, Qingyang Palace of Chengdu

Lion playing with a ball,
screen-wall stucco sculpture, Xianyou, Fujian

Qilin bringing luck, screen-wall stucco sculpture, Chaozhou, Guangdong

Door-head stucco sculpture, Liu Family Manor, Dayi, Sichuan

Door head stucco sculpture, Liu Family Manor, Dayi, Sichuan

Hanging fish, pediment stucco sculpture,
former Cai family residence, Quanzhou, Fujian

*Recao* design, pediment stucco sculpture,
former Cai family residence, Quanzhou, Fujian

Door-head stucco sculpture, Hu Family Compound,
Taishun, Zhejiang

Eave-wall stucco sculpture, former Chen family residence,
Chenghai, Guangdong

The 12 animals representing the 12 years of birth, eave-wall stucco sculpture,
Wangjianglou Pavilion, Chengdu

Lucky star shining on high, gable-wall stucco sculpture,
Chaozhou, Guangdong

Pediment on rooftop, stucco sculpture, former Chen family residence,
Chenghai, Guangdong

Eave-wall stucco sculpture, Foshan, Guangdong

## Magpie on a Plum Branch

The magpie is a sign of happiness. Plum in Chinese is pronounced "*mei*," similar to the word for "brow." So the design signifying happiness appears high on the brow, symbolizing that happiness is imminent.

## Mandarin Ducks and Lotus

Mandarin ducks, always together in pairs, are often compared to affectionate couples.

Magpie on a plum branch, stucco sculpture, Baomoyuan, Fanyu, Guangdong

Mandarin ducks and lotus, stucco sculpture, Baomoyuan, Fanyu, Guangdong

*Bogu* design, stucco sculpture, Fujian

### Muke Zhai

*Muke Zhai* is a famous episode in an opera. It tells of a marriage between two hostile rivals. Yang Zongbao follows the orders of his father to battle Mu Guiying, a daughter of a mountain-stronghold owner, in order to acquire a piece of magical wood. However, he is defeated and captured by Mu Guiying. Yet Mu gradually falls in love with Yang Zongbao, and the two marry in the end.

Beautiful lady, eave-wall stucco sculpture, Mazu Temple, Foshan, Guangdong

Theatrical figures, rooftop stucco sculpture,
Shuangliu, Chengdu

Stucco Sculpture

Figures from *Muke Zhai*, rooftop stucco sculpture,
Shuangliu, Chengdu

Two dragons playing with a ball, stucco sculptured ridge decoration,
Wuhou Temple, Chengdu

Treasure vase, stucco sculptured ridge decoration,
Shibao Village in Zhongxian, Chognqing

Theatrical figures, stucco sculptured ridge decoration,
Mazu Temple, Foshan, Guangdong

Simplified dragon design, stucco sculptured ridge decoration,
Kaiyuan Temple, Chaozhou, Guangdong

Auspicious birds and animals, stucco sculptured ridge decoration,
Lord Guan Temple, Dongshan, Fujian

Flower and bird design, stucco sculptured main ridge decoration,
Kaiyuan Temple, Quanzhou, Fujian

Lion and flower design, stucco sculptured main ridge decoration,
Kaiyuan Temple, Quanzhou, Fujian

*Stucco Sculpture*

Line pattern, stucco sculptured ridge decoration,
Mazu Temple, Foshan, Guangdong

Auspicious birds and animals, stucco sculptured ridge decoration,
Lord Guan Temple, Dongshan, Fujian

## Da Ji (Great Luck)

The design mainly features a rooster or a rooster with a child on its back. It is said that a rooster is an auspicious fowl that can drive away evil and is noted for its five virtues: literacy, militancy, courage, benevolence and trustworthiness. As the word is pronounced the same as "auspiciousness" in Chinese, it also represents auspiciousness.

Rooster, stucco sculptured ridge decoration, Lord Guan Temple, Dongshan, Fujian

## Deer

Deer is upheld as an auspicious animal in China. As "deer" is pronounced "*lu*," similar to "salary" or "remuneration" in Chinese, it has become a symbol of wealth. In ancient times, the white deer was regarded as the most precious for celestial beings to sit on, so it also signifies longevity.

Deer, stucco sculptured ridge decoration, Lord Guan Temple, Dongshan, Fujian

Theatrical figures, stucco sculptured ridge decoration,
Lord Guan Temple, Dongshan, Fujian

GLAZE

# Glaze

Glaze decoration is a major feature of Chinese architecture. It began to be applied in the 4th century, and was applied to the entire house roof by the 7th century. The application found its way into major structures after the 10th century. Since the 14th century, the glaze colors developed from yellow, blue and green into a dozen colors and hues, including jade green, peacock blue, amethystine, light yellow, black and white, making glaze works more and more expressive. Historically, Beijing and Shanxi as well as Qufu in Shandong have enjoyed quite a name for their use of glaze. In feudal patriarchal society, glaze could be used to decorate only imperial structures and temples. In folk architecture, glaze was mainly used to decorate the screen walls, wall face and rooftops.

Peony, screen-wall glaze, Longxing Temple, Zhengding, Hebei

Rinceau pattern, screen-wall glaze, Zhang Fei Temple, Langzhong, Sichuan

Two dragons playing with a ball, screen-wall glaze, Mazu Temple, Foshan, Guangdong

Two dragons playing with a ball,
glazed central flower, Longxing Temple,
Zhengding, Hebei

Dragon design, screen-wall glaze, Taihuiguan Temple, Jingzhou, Hubei

## Liu He Tong Chun (Spring Everywhere)

Liu he refers to Heaven, Earth and the four directions. Liu he tong chun means "Everywhere is Spring under Heaven." There are two compositions of the design. One mainly features the combination of deer, crane, pine and Chinese toon. The other features the combination of deer, crane and officials. Deer and crane are both symbols of longevity as liu is homophone of six directions, and He of harmony.

Deer and cranes, screen-wall glaze, Kaiyuan Temple, Quanzhou, Fujian

Qilin bringing luck, screen-wall glaze, Kaiyuan Temple, Quanzhou, Fujian

Phoenix and peony, wall-face glaze, Chenghuang Temple, Sanyuan, Shaanxi

Two dragons playing with a ball, gable-wall glaze, Wutaishan Mountain, Shanxi

Phoenix and peony, wall-face glaze, Shihu Garden, Weifang, Shandong

Glaze decoration for a roof ridge, Chenghuang Temple, Sanyuan, Shaanxi

Double dragon and a treasure bottle, glaze decoration for the roof ridge,
Lusheng Temple, Huangliangmeng, Handan City, Hebei

Auspicious animals and treasure bottle, glaze decoration for the roof ridge,
Longxing Temple, Zhengding, Hebei

## 图书在版编目（CIP）数据

民间砖雕：英文／蓝先琳编著；金绍卿译．
—北京：外文出版社，2008
（中国民间文化遗产）
ISBN 978-7-119-04672-3

I. 民… II. ①蓝… ②金… III. 砖—装饰雕塑—民间工艺—中国—
英文 IV. J314.9

### 中国版本图书馆 CIP 数据核字（2008）第 086545 号

| | |
|---|---|
| **出版策划：** | 李振国 |
| **英文翻译：** | 金绍卿 |
| **英文审定：** | Kris Sri Bhaggiyadatta　May Yee　王明杰 |
| **责任编辑：** | 杨春燕 |
| **文案编辑：** | 刘芳念 |
| **装帧设计：** | 黎　红 |
| **印刷监制：** | 韩少乙 |

本书由中国轻工业出版社授权出版

## 民间砖雕

蓝先琳　编著

\*

© 外文出版社

**出　　版：**

外文出版社出版（中国北京百万庄大街24号）
邮政编码　100037　www.flp.com.cn

**印　　刷：**

北京外文印刷厂

**发　　行：**

中国国际图书贸易总公司发行（中国北京车公庄西路 35 号）
北京邮政信箱第 399 号　邮政编码：100044

2008 年（小 16 开）第 1 版
2008 年第 1 版第 1 次印刷
（英）
ISBN 978-7-119-04672-3
09800（平）
　　　　　　　　　　　　　　　　　　　建议上架：
85-E-644 P
　　　　　　　　　　　　　　　　　　　原版／对外汉语